Cure

or

Cover Up?

Henry W. Wright

4178 Crest Highway
Thomaston, Georgia 30286

www.beinhealth.com

EAN: 978-1-934680-15-5

Copyright Notice

Disclaimer

This ministry does not seek to be in conflict with any medical or psychiatric practices nor do we seek to be in conflict with any church and its religious doctrines, beliefs or practices. We are not a part of medicine or psychology, yet we work to make them more effective, rather than working against them. We believe many human problems are fundamentally spiritual with associated physiological and psychological manifestations. This information is intended for your general knowledge only. Information is presented only to give insight into disease, its problems and its possible solutions in the area of disease eradication and/or prevention. It is not a substitute for medical advice or treatment for specific medical conditions or disorders. You should seek prompt medical care for any specific health issues. Treatment modalities around your specific health issues are between you and your physician.

We are not responsible for a person's disease, nor are we responsible for his/her healing. All we can do is share what we see about a problem. We are not professionals; we are not healers. We are administering the Scriptures, and what they say about this subject, along with what the medical and scientific communities have also observed in line with this insight. There is no guarantee that any person will be healed or any disease be prevented. The fruits of this teaching will come forth out of the relationship between the person and God based on these insights given and applied. This ministry is patterned after the following scriptures: 2 Corinthians 5:18-20; 1 Corinthians 12; Ephesians 4; Mark 16:15-20.

Preface

This booklet was developed from a teaching to a live audience and has been kept in a conversational format. It is designed to reach a personal level with the reader rather than present a structured, theological presentation. Many times the reader will feel that Henry Wright is talking directly to him or her. The frequent use of the pronoun you is meant to penetrate the human heart for conviction, not for accusation.

Table of Contents

Now the works of the flesh are manifest,
which are *THESE*;
Adultery, fornication, uncleanness,
lasciviousness, Idolatry,

Witchcraft*,

hatred, variance, emulations,
wrath, strife, seditions,
heresies, Envyings, murders,
drunkenness, revellings, and such like...

Galatians 5:19-21

*Witchcraft is *Pharmakeia* in the original Greek

Cure or Cover Up?

Introduction

There is a lot of misunderstanding as to the definition of "witchcraft" and "sorcery." Most Christians believe these are things practiced by pagan cultures either in the days of antiquity or by modern witches and practitioners of Wicca.

The word "witchcraft" is found in a list of the works of the flesh in Galatians. Many people are bound in some way by the powers of witchcraft (or *pharmakeia* in the original Greek) and sorcery without even realizing it. In order to understand these words, we will let the Word of God define them. That way it is not just an opinion; it is the correct understanding we should have as Believers.

Let's take a look at what Paul is writing to the Galatians.

> **Now the works of the flesh are manifest...**
> Galatians 5:19

The word "manifest" means something invisible can now be seen. There is one invisible kingdom now manifesting in the visible kingdom, and it does so through humans — or it wants to.

> **¹⁹Now the works of the flesh are manifest, which are these; Adultery, fornication, uncleanness, lasciviousness,**

[20]Idolatry, witchcraft, hatred, variance, emulations, wrath, strife, seditions, heresies,

[21]Envyings, murders, drunkenness, revellings, and such like: of the which I tell you before, as I have also told you in time past, that they which do such things shall not inherit the kingdom of God.

Galatians 5:19-21

When I first read "they which do such things shall not inherit the kingdom of God," I did not think there was a chance for anyone to ever make it! Most Christians I saw had one or more of these things currently active in their lives.

These works of the flesh include many things—from adultery to reveling. Take this list individually and you might be surprised to see wrath and strife along with murder. Many people do not really equate strife with sin; for them it is just a psychological exercise. But the Bible places strife right along with adultery and murder!

In some families, churches and sectors of society, strife seems to be a fashionable exercise of recreation. It is just a thing you do. Tormenting your brother should not be something you do!

I was concerned about the statement: "those who do such things shall not inherit the kingdom of God." So I looked up "do" in the *Strong's Concordance* and found an interesting definition. The word "do" in the *Strong's* means those that habitually practice a thing, as opposed to one single act.

Now that brings me to a defining position. There is a difference between Christians who habitually practice one of these issues as a way of life without conscience and without turning away from it—and those who *occasionally* do such things.

"Occasional" means you fall into it and fall out of it, fall into it and fall out of it. You can fall into strife and fall back out of it, and you will still inherit the kingdom of God.

However, if you are in one of these areas temporarily, and you *continue in it after the knowledge of the truth*, you're in trouble. If you habitually practice some of these rudimentary issues of the works of the flesh as a way of life, then you "shall not inherit the kingdom of God."

Those who habitually practice sin shall not inherit the kingdom of God

That is a pretty serious statement! Do you know what is really interesting about it? This statement is in Galatians—the great book against legalism that establishes our freedom in Christ. But grace and mercy is not a license to sin. Do we sin more that grace might more abound? God forbid!

> [1]What shall we say then? Shall we continue in sin, that grace may abound?
>
> [2]God forbid...
>
> Romans 6:1-2

Grace and mercy is not a license to sin and there is a consequence for the habitual practice of sin.

Witchcraft

The word I want to take you to in Galatians 5:20 is "witchcraft." Now I have been around Christians for awhile and when you talk to them about certain words in the Bible every word becomes generic. They don't do their word studies. The word "witchcraft" is also in the Old Testament, in 1 Samuel.

> For rebellion is as the sin of witchcraft, and stubbornness is as iniquity and idolatry. Because thou hast rejected the word of the LORD, he hath also rejected thee from being king.
>
> 1 Samuel 15:23

Because it says, "For rebellion is as the sin of witchcraft," some people think rebellion in itself is the only meaning of the word witchcraft. But don't make that mistake!

Some assume "witchcraft" only refers to the pagan custom of casting spells and the worship of mythological figures. I have been pastor for many years, and sometimes I ask Christians to define witchcraft. Probably 99.9 percent of those responses is this: witchcraft means casting spells and worshipping false gods.

The word witchcraft is only found one time in the New Testament. You have to be careful when you are transliterating or translating from different languages into English. When you go from Hebrew to English it is not the same as when you go from Greek to English. In other words, do not assume that the English word "witchcraft" in the Old Testament has the same meaning as it does in the New Testament.

5

Almost 9,000 different Hebrew words were used to write the Old Testament, but less than 6,000 Greek words were used to write the New Testament. In the Hebrew language there is a word for nearly every vein of thought. On the other hand, Greek, like English, has words with more than one meaning.

Take the word "flesh" for example. It can mean an animal that you eat, like a chicken. It can mean your human body or it can mean Satan's nature in you. So when Paul said to "crucify" the flesh, he did not mean to go and kill a chicken. He did not mean you should go and kill yourself. He meant, "Kill what's in you that is not of God."

Some people say, "Well, it's just my body; it's just my flesh acting out."

It is not their flesh acting independently that does the evil act, is it? Paul says, "Now then it is no more I that do it, but the sin that dwells within me."

> **15**For that which I do I allow not: for what I would, that do I not; but what I hate, that do I.

> **16**If then I do that which I would not, I consent unto the law that *it is* good.

> **17**Now then it is no more I that do it, but sin that dwelleth in me.
>
> Romans 7:15-17

Sin thinks; your body does not think. Your body is just your mobile home. According to Scripture, Sin is a being. It has a body and, when you participate with Sin, you are following Sin as a servant follows his master.

6

> Knowing this, that our old man is crucified with him, that the body of sin might be destroyed, that henceforth we should not serve sin.
>
> Romans 6:6

Let's go back to the word "witchcraft" in Galatians. It is *Strong's* #5331, out of #5332, the Greek word *"pharmakeia."* Understanding the root word is something we all need to do as we study the Word of God.

Pharmakeia, #5331, is taken from the root word #5332 which is *"pharmakeus."* It is translated into English as "witchcraft." The literal meaning here is a drug, a spell-giving potion, a druggist, a pharmacist or a poison. *"Pharmakeia"* literally means medication, or pharmacy by extension.

Medication

Witchcraft in Galatians 5 means medications as prescribed by a pharmacist. Now, please understand that I am not against doctors—there is a place for them. Neither am I against medications—there is a place for them also. But when you use medication to give you ease or to produce an altered state of soul or biological consciousness, your enemy goes free.

While you are chemically managed and altered, the old enemy of Sin in your life is not dealt with. *That is why pharmakeia is sin.*

BETA-BLOCKERS

Most people take medications because they need relief. The majority of those taken for pain are beta-blockers. These drugs shut down the pathway of pain. You still have the pain; you just don't know it. So it is an occultic delusion of safety. As long as you take the medication, you do not feel the pain.

In high blood pressure, stress causes a stiffening of the cell membrane, which produces a narrowing of the arteries. This creates a back-up in the blood flow: the blood wants to flow through, but the opening is now narrow because of cell membrane semi-rigidity. It begins to back up and that creates a higher pressure—which is known as High Blood Pressure, or Hypertension.

When they feel scattered and smothered, people go to their doctor. The first thing he does is check blood pressure, and sure enough, it's high! So he says, "No problem. I'll give you some High Blood Pressure medication."

He gives them a beta-blocker which lies to the body, short-circuiting the sympathetic nervous system pathway causing the problem. That way, the mechanism causing cell membrane semi-rigidity will be broken. The membranes, or walls, of the veins and arteries are released and begin to relax and open up. The blood begins to flow normally and pressure returns to normal. In the medical community, High Blood Pressure is considered to be a stress disorder.

BYPASSING THE PENALTY

Is stress Sin? Yes, because it represents Fear. According to Romans 14, whatsoever is not of faith is Sin.

> And he that doubteth is damned if he eat, because *he eateth* not of faith: for whatsoever *is* not of faith is sin.
> Romans 14:23

Now we have a dilemma as people of God! Since fear, anxiety and stress are the opposite of faith and peace, they represent the operation of Sin in our lives. Ask yourself this question: Is it God's will that I deal with and remove the stress that is Fear? Or should I allow it to stay while I enter an altered state of chemical consciousness to pretend I don't have the problem?

Do you think God wants you delivered from Fear? Psalm 34 says the Lord delivers you of all your fears.

> I sought the LORD, and he heard me, and delivered me from all my fears.
> Psalm 34:4

When you take a drug, it is an attempt to artificially bypass the penalty of the curse of disobedience without taking responsibility for the Sin that caused the physiological problem. Now you have two sins: the original one called Fear and the second one called witchcraft to maintain yourself. Your enemy is now laughing his head off at you!

Now you can understand why Paul is calling this a "work of the flesh." Many times medications are used to circumvent the curse. They give you ease from the effects of the curse while you never, ever deal with the lack of sanctification in that area of your life. That is why a drug is occultic; it offers itself as if it were the solution.

Medications can be occultic solutions to our lack of sanctification

The Bible says even the priest and the prophet have erred.

> But they also have erred through wine, and through strong drink are out of the way; the priest and the prophet have erred through strong drink, they are swallowed up of wine, they are out of the way through strong drink; they err in vision, they stumble in judgment.
> Isaiah 28:7

"The priest and the prophet have erred, and they have only healed the hurt of the daughter of my people slightly saying, Peace, peace and there is no peace."

> They have healed also the hurt of the daughter of my people slightly, saying, Peace, peace; when there is no peace.
> Jeremiah 6:14

Jesus said,

Peace I leave with you, my peace I give unto you: not as the world giveth, give I unto you. Let not your heart be troubled, neither let it be afraid.

John 14:27

Overcoming Sin

May I submit to you that Prozac is a bad substitute for the Holy Spirit? It is a chemical peace. Your enemy knows how to throw you into chemical imbalance. Your enemy not only knows how to destroy your immune system, he knows how to alter your body's chemistry. He knows how to produce pain.

Your enemy knows how to alter neurotransmitter balances so they are either too high or too low. You either have a serotonin deficiency or a serotonin oversecretion. You either have a dopamine deficiency or dopamine oversecretion. Your body chemistry goes out of whack based on whether or not your mind is fixed and stayed on the Lord; whether or not you are listening to that other gospel of Satan coming through your mind and your spirit.

There is a place for painkillers because there are things that happen in life and pain is no fun. But many times people are taking painkillers because the pain is psychogenic, originating in the mind or the emotions. Mental conflict produces the pain, not an injury.

I deal with more than two dozen types of psychogenic pain. Fibromyalgia is one of them and migraines are another.

Paul identifies *pharmakeia* as two things. First, it is sin. And second, it is a work of the flesh. The scripture says, "Those that do such things shall not inherit the kingdom of God." If you are being managed by a drug for anxiety disorders, then I would say you have a spirit of Fear.

I think it is time to get right with God! If we have fallen this far with the diseases of Egypt and the sorcerers of Egypt to avoid the living God and what creation should look like, it is not God's fault. It is mankind's fault.

Deuteronomy chapter 7 outlines the blessings of obedience: He will take away all sickness and put none of the evil diseases of Egypt upon us.

> [11]Thou shalt therefore keep the commandments, and the statutes, and the judgments, which I command thee this day, to do them.

> [12]Wherefore it shall come to pass, if ye hearken to these judgments, and keep, and do them, that the LORD thy God shall keep unto thee the covenant and the mercy which he sware unto thy fathers:

> [13]And he will love thee, and bless thee, and multiply thee: he will also bless the fruit of thy womb, and the fruit of thy land, thy corn, and thy wine, and thine oil, the increase of thy kine, and the flocks of thy sheep, in the land which he sware unto thy fathers to give thee.

> [14]Thou shalt be blessed above all people: there shall not be male or female barren among you, or among your cattle.

> [15]And the LORD will take away from thee all sickness, and will put none of the evil diseases of Egypt, which thou knowest, upon thee; but will lay them upon all *them* that hate thee.
>
> Deuteronomy 7:11-15

It is time for us, as people of God, to establish the kingdom of God in the earth. Otherwise, we will continue to establish the kingdom of Satan, offering that for the future of mankind. Whether or not we—collectively or personally—win this battle, now is the time to start preaching the gospel of our God, *even if we never walk in it ourselves.*

God does not judge you on the basis of your sin. He does not judge you around whether you do have sin or don't have sin. Why? Because your entrance into heaven is not based on being sinless when you die.

I can see us Christians going down our checklists as we are gasping for our last breath. We are still saved by faith! God judges us first on the basis of our attitudes toward sin, not whether or not we have overcome it.

Are you in the process of working out your salvation, being convicted because the Holy Spirit is dealing with you? Do you hate the stuff that binds you? Then obviously you are accepted of God because the Holy Spirit is working in you.

As long as He is there convicting you, you're okay! If He has withdrawn from your life, then you are in trouble. King David said in Psalm 51 his greatest fear was God would take His Holy Spirit from him.

> **Cast me not away from thy presence; and take not thy holy spirit from me.**
>
> Psalm 51:11

Let's take two Christians with the same sin. One hates it and the other loves it. One is doing the sin and hates it, while the other one habitually practices the sin and couldn't care less. Both are Christians. One is accepted of God and the other is rejected of God.

This kind of knowledge is designed to develop your hatred for sin and bring your understanding into focus. You need to be prepared to take a stand against things which are not of God—against whatever is putting you in bondage and stealing your life and your money.

15

A recent national statistic says the percentage of money given back to God in tithes and offerings in America is 2.7 percent. I will tell you where the rest is going: to the sorcerer and the debt load! Malachi 3:8 tells us that we rob God in tithes and offerings.

> Will a man rob God? Yet ye have robbed me. But ye say, Wherein have we robbed thee? In tithes and offerings.
>
> Malachi 3:8

One of the blocks to healing in *A More Excellent Way*™ is robbing God of tithes and offerings. Some might say, "I don't believe in tithes. I'm not under the law." Abraham paid tithes to Melchizedek, yet the law was not given until 435 years later!

Accidental Death in Medicine

The next area of our discussion not only covers the problem with the pharmaceutical industry, but also the dilemma with our physician base. Knowledge comes so wisdom can move you ahead. Knowledge ties the past to the present. But wisdom takes you from the present to the future. So we are going to mix knowledge with wisdom to take you into the future.

Several years ago a pastor sent me this story called "Doctors and Accidental Gun Deaths'" from the *Benton County News Tribune*, November 17, 1999.

The number of physicians in the US is 700,000. Accidental deaths caused by physicians per year: 120,000. Accidental deaths per physician: 0.171, or 17.1 percent. The source of this information: Department of Health and Human Services.

The number of gun owners in the US: 80,000,000. Number of accidental gun deaths per year, all age groups: 1,500. Accidental deaths per gun owner: 0.0000188.

Statistically, doctors are approximately 9,000 times more dangerous than gun owners. Remember, not everyone has a gun, but everyone has at least one doctor.

The note from the pastor said, "Please alert your friends to this alarming threat."[1]

---

[1] Miller, E., personal communication, June 27, 2001.

TOP TEN KILLERS

Let me tell you about the top ten killers of people in America. This information is taken from *USA Today*, November 30, 1999.[2]

- The number 1 killer of people in America is Heart Disease.

- The number 2 killer of people in America is Cancer.

- The number 3 killer of people in America is Strokes.

That would include aneurysms, which are congesting or exploding embolisms.

- The number 4 killer of people in America is death from prescription drugs

These deaths are caused by the drugs being prescribed by physicians! Death in America from the use of illegal drugs does not even make the top ten! I think our war on drugs needs to be redefined quickly.

- Number 5 is Chronic Obstructive Lung Disease.

- Number 6 is accidents.

- Number 7 is Pneumonia and Influenza.

- Number 8 is from medical mistakes at the hand of the attending physician.

---

[2] Davis, B., (1999, November 30). Medical mistakes 8th top killer. *USAToday*.

- Number 9 is Diabetes.

- Number 10 is HIV/AIDS.

Of the top ten killers of people in America today, number 4 is prescription drugs and number 8 is mistakes made by the doctor. Accidental deaths by physicians is 17.1 percent! Now you understand why I am concerned.

Let me give you another statistic found in a press release from the *Anchorage Daily News*, July 24, 1999. Merck and Co., a leading US pharmaceutical company, reported their second quarter net income rose 12 percent. That is just for three months, not a whole year.

In just three months Merck sold more medicines for High Cholesterol, High Blood Pressure and Asthma than the previous quarter. That statistic represents net income for that quarter, not gross sales. Their net profit was 1.48 billion dollars in just one quarter.

God does not want you to be maintained by some kind of medication for High Cholesterol. He would rather have you finally accept His love and accept yourself in the new birth.

God does not want you to be maintained by a drug for High Blood Pressure. He wants you to be free from the stress and anxiety producing the problem. God does not want you to be on Asthma medication. He wants you to be released from the Fear of Abandonment issues producing the Asthma.

Just Say No

Dr. Julian Whitaker has an article in *Health and Healing*, October 2000,[3] entitled 'Just Say No to Drugs.' The article states:

> According to an article published in the *Journal of the American Medical Association (JAMA)* in July 2000, at least 225,000 Americans die each year from the side effects of medical care...

That would be from things that go wrong!

> ...including an astounding 106,000 to non-error adverse effects of drugs (meaning these drugs were used as prescribed by physicians). Other than heart disease and cancer, nothing—not stroke, diabetes, pulmonary disease, AIDS, accidents, murder or illegal drugs—kills more people than the medical industry. And the worst culprit is FDA-approved drugs.

But we run there quickly! Do you know why? We have Fear of disease and Fear of dying. We have been bewitched in our Sin and that is what sorcery and witchcraft—which are occultism—do.

The article continues:

> Americans give millions of public and private dollars to organizations that seek cures for cancer, heart disease, diabetes and other killers. A significant portion of our taxes fund highway patrol officers, firefighters, safety inspectors and others devoted to

---

[3] Whitaker, J., (2000). Just say no to drugs. *Health and Healing, 10* (10), 1-3.

curtailing accidents. Billions of dollars have been spent on the "war on drugs." Yet for reasons which I cannot fathom, one of the most significant threats to our health—the real drug problem in this country—is ignored altogether.

There is no public uprising to get to the bottom of these unnecessary and preventable drug-related fatalities. Instead of being vilified, the entities behind the third-leading cause of death in our country are the heroes of the evening news, the darlings of Wall Street, and the chums of Congressmen. Furthermore, the FDA, the government agency entrusted with regulating this industry, ignores blatant conflicts of interest, turns a blind eye to fraudulent testing, and approves record numbers of new drugs, many of which are subsequently pulled from the market because they maim and kill people.

Why do we ignore the obvious? The multibillion-dollar drug companies have penetrated our society to such a degree that we've come to look to drugs as the answer for everything that ails us. Although much of the blame lies with physicians and the pharmaceutical companies that court them to the tune of $13,000 per doctor per year, patients don't get off scot-free. We want those magic bullets that absolve us of taking responsibility for our own health.

This trend has accelerated now that the pharmaceutical industry has been given the FDA's blessing to advertise drugs directly to consumers. By glorifying their products with slick marketing campaigns, glossy magazine ads and prime time commercials, they create a false impression that prescription drugs are panaceas with an unblemished history of success and safety. And we swallow every word of their advertising hype. Thanks to this relatively new and ominous development, patients themselves have begun asking their doctors for the latest drugs by name, and doctors usually oblige by writing a prescription.

The next headline of Dr. Whitaker's article reads: *A Witch's Brew of Drugs*. That matches "witchcraft," doesn't it?

Not only do we have a problem with adults, but more kids are on prescribed drugs. More than 200,000 children under the age of 18 are now on prescription drugs, most of them anxiety drugs or serotonin drug enhancers.

We have become a nation drugged to avoid taking responsibility for what produces ill health!

TEENS AND RITALIN

Teens are using Ritalin to get high and it has become the drug of choice in colleges. Ritalin is a very dangerous drug. It has been given for Hyperactivity and Attention-Deficit/Hyperactivity Disorder (ADHD) and has resulted in over 50 percent of its users, beginning in childhood, to be at odds with the law and to end up in prison.

Ritalin creates a wide range of psychotic behavior. Prozac is not far behind. Dr. Whitaker begins to take Prozac and its dangers on for size. In most of the psychotic murders that we have had in America, including those at Columbine High School in Colorado and all the rest you've heard about, those individuals were on Prozac. The side effects of Prozac include hostility, violence and psychotic behavior.

PRESCRIPTION ABUSE

Eleven percent of all women in America over age 59 are addicted to, or abuse, prescription drugs. Nearly 2,000,000 people in America are now taking Ritalin. One in 5 prescriptions at the college level for Ritalin is abused because it is used as an alternative kind of speed. It sort of "keeps you going." It is broken up and used almost like cocaine.

The other drug getting quite a bit of attention in America is OxyContin. The town of Hazard, Kentucky, has over 100 addicts to this one drug. Doctors are being arrested for prescribing OxyContin without any regard to the side effects. When used as a pain killer, it is one of the most dangerously addictive drugs in the world.

Herbs and Supplements

As a pastor, I'm really concerned about herbs and supplements. Most of them have never been tested properly. This is from *InteliHealth*, home to Johns Hopkins Health Information: Health News. It is dated March, 1999.

Scientists at Johns Hopkins have uncovered a new worry about some of the most popular herbal remedies: the possibility that they could cause infertility or genetically damage sperm.

Many women who are pregnant or are trying to conceive carefully avoid taking prescription and even over-the-counter medications for fear they could endanger their chances of a healthy pregnancy.

But herbs and other dietary supplements are advertised as "natural," with the implication that they're safe, non-drug remedies. In fact, many powerful prescription drugs were derived from plants, and many of the herbs sold in health-food stores and supermarkets also can have powerful, medicine-like actions — and side effects.

The new study by researchers at Loma Linda University suggests that the side effects of some popular herbs — St. John's wort, echinacea and gingko — could include blocking conception. The study also uncovered suggestions of genetic damage to sperm, raising questions of whether such changes could cause problems for a resulting baby.

St. John's wort completely blocked the ability of sperm to penetrate eggs. Echinacea and gingko reduced that ability. Eggs treated with gingko were visibly degenerated.

25

Echinacea and St. John's wort produced DNA changes reducing sperm viability and sperm treated with St. John's Wort showed a mutation of a gene called BRCA-1, a mutation that, when found in grown women, is associated with an increased risk of breast and ovarian cancer."[4]

Another research article from *IntelliHealth* is entitled, "Dietary Supplements Are No Substitute for Proper Diet".[5] It states: "More older Americans—the people most at risk of cancer—said they're popping unproven dietary supplements in a quest for tumor-fighting nutrients than trying to eat more cancer-protective foods."

That's why the food supplement industry is worth $40 billion a year!

We are in so much fear of disease we will try anything. The average person in America is spending between $300 and $500 per month on herbs, dietary supplements and other things because of the Fear of disease and Fear of dying.

---

[4] *Herbal-Infertility Link Explored.* (1999, March26) *Health News* [On-Line]. Available: http://www.intelihealth.com/IH/ihtIH?t=333&st=333&r= EMIHC000& c=216841 [1999, April 20]

[5] *Dietary Supplements No Substitute For Proper Diet.* (2000, September 5). *Health News* [On-Line].   Available: http://www.intelihealth.com/IH/ihtPrint/ EMIHC000/333/7228/296661/html?k=basePrint

Bad Mixers

Discover Magazine talks about bad mixers.[6] People who combine certain herbal medicines and/or prescription drugs may be putting themselves at considerable risk. Someone can have 5 diseases, go to 5 specialists, be given 5 different prescription drugs and one hand does not know what the other hand is doing!

There are certain combinations of drugs that are lethal. The average person will not know what combinations can potentially produce death. I want to help you become more knowledgeable about drug combinations.

Here is a list of 10 drugs that, when taken together, could cause injury or death:

Seldane taken with Erythromycin

Mevacore and Lopid

Coumadin and Tagamet

Calan and Duraquin

Theo-Dur and Tagamet

Digoxin or Lanoxin and Calan

Prozac and Dilantin

Halcion and Erythromycin

Eldepryl and Norpramin

Tagamet and Dilantin

---

[6] Glauslusz, J., (2000, April). Bad Mixers. *Discover.*

Drugs combined with herbs can be equally lethal. St. John's wort, a popular mood-lifting herbal remedy, when taken with antidepressants such as Prozac, may increase the risk of confusion, nausea and diarrhea. These are all symptoms of an excess in the brain of the neurotransmitter serotonin. So you would not want to take St. John's wort and Prozac together!

Gingko can trigger bleeding in people taking Warfarin, a drug that reduces the risk of blood clots. Yohimbine, an anti-impotence herb, can produce hypertension when combined with tricyclic antidepressants.

Herbal medicines alone can be trouble as well. Asian herbal medicines have been found to be contaminated with lead or arsenic and some have been doctored with drugs such as steroids.

The Food and Drug Administration does not regulate the use or sale of herbs. *Blade's Wire* indicates Vitamin C overdoses may harm the body's cells. The FDA does not approve supplements or regulate their advertising. So you have to be careful of some of the ad copy. Some results they offer you are unproven.

In fact, many of these companies are under litigation for misrepresenting mind-improvement as one of the herb's benefits. They say the supplements improve memory and concentration, help increase serotonin levels, are immune enhancers and may help reduce cholesterol. They make claims for bone health and cartilage rejuvenation and repair. The claims are endless!

The dean of a medical school has said he is concerned less about the manufacturer; the real disappointment is the pharmacists. He wonders if many pharmacists have given up their role as health professionals—maybe they're no longer in control of the store. Maybe they're just behind the counter and there is an attitude that "anything goes" in front of the counter because it has to be sold.

Migraines

The following is a quote from *USA Today*, July 5, 2001, article entitled "Doctors Step Out, Drug Salesmen Step In."

> It's no longer what your doctor says. It's what the drug companies are saying you need. You can pick up almost any magazine and find several advertisements for a variety of drugs in it. Most of them are very well produced and deceivingly appealing to the eye. Take as an example, a center page glossy with a lady breaking into freedom from migraines. Migraines are a shattering life experience, and the promotion of a drug called Imitrex lures you into the lie that this would solve all your problems.

I have taught and written in *A More Excellent Way*™ about migraines. I am completely convinced migraines have a spiritual root, which involves anxiety and conflict. These conflicts may be self-with-self or conflict with someone else.

THE CAUSE

Migraines are not caused by the conflict itself, but by the conflict you have with yourself *about the conflict*. That produces a lowered level of serotonin which always comes when you do not like yourself or when you are in doubt about yourself.

Then Fear comes which releases an excessive secretion of histamine. Serotonin is a vasoconstrictor. At proper levels, it keeps the blood vessels in place and at the correct width. When levels of serotonin are lowered, the vessels expand. And something else happens with lowered levels: you go into anxiety. This causes an excessive release of histamine which is a vasodilator.

IMITREX

So now you have a migraine. What will your doctor give you? Probably the drug Imitrex. The Physician's Desk Reference, or PDR, lists the pharmaceutical mechanisms and pharmacology of Imitrex. It is an incredible thing!

Did you know that Imitrex is now the drug of choice for treating migraines? In about 75 percent of all cases it stops migraines, but it does not prevent them. Imitrex is a compound drug. It is a serotonin enhancer and an antihistamine. Serotonin and histamine are what are called "agonists."

Have you ever seen the little black and white terrier magnets? If you put the two magnets together, they spin around and go the other way. Because they are polar opposites, they push each other away.

It's like that with serotonin and histamine. They cannot be in the same place at the same time. One of them has to give way to the other. When people are in a state of conflict, they do not like themselves anymore. They distrust their own thoughts about this issue of conflict and serotonin levels dip. That allows histamine to gain ascendancy and causes vasodilation.

Imitrex acts as an antihistamine, which means it is a beta-blocker. It shuts off the secretion of histamine coming out of anxiety and Fear. When the oversecretion of histamine is stopped, serotonin is enhanced. Imitrex, then, is a serotonin enhancer like Prozac. It does not increase the value or the quantity of serotonin; it just keeps serotonin in circulation longer.

Now you feel good about yourself and the pineal gland releases serotonin. You feel good in your spirit and soul and your body agrees.

Prozac

When you do not feel good about yourself, the pineal gland shuts down the value system. You do not have as much serotonin in circulation. You don't feel good about yourself in your spirit, soul or body. You now feel uneasy because you have all these biological mis-firings going on.

So you go to the doctor and say, "I really don't feel well."

He says, "Let me give you some Prozac."

Prozac shuts down the ports in the dendrite of the nerve. The serotonin that has been released now comes back into the ports to be recycled. But there's a problem. More is needed and it needs to stay in circulation longer. Since the port is closed, the serotonin bounces off and goes back into circulation. Prozac allows more serotonin to be in circulation and you feel good!

Did Prozac solve the fact that you did not like yourself? No! It lied to you. It says you now feel good about yourself; but if you think about it in your heart, you still do not like yourself. This is occultic, delusional bewitchment. But you feel better, don't you? You are just a bewitched, feel-better Christian.

Well, what is wrong with that? Is that who God created you to be? Did He create you delusional and bewitched, pretending you do not have a spiritual problem?

Imitrex is an antihistamine and removes the histamines from your system. Take it and your serotonin levels come back up where they belong. Since serotonin is a vasoconstrictor, the diameter of the blood vessels begins to shrink back to normal and the migraine is over.

We have been able to help hundreds of people who get frequent migraines. They don't have them anymore! They have been taught how to understand their battle. Now when they recognize their precursors for a headache, they go to war and God meets them in it. They can shut the migraine down right in the middle of the precursor.

This is true spiritual warfare — not shadowboxing. You need to know your enemy. You need to know exactly how he is creating a malfunction and where he is doing it. That is what God wants you to know.

PROZAC, THE HOLY SPIRIT SUBSTITUTE

Let's talk about Prozac. It has some very dangerous side effects. In fact, in *Discover* Magazine, July 2001, there is a whole section on Prozac. It is called *The Serotonin Surprise.*[7] Prozac produces an altered state of consciousness and is now the first illegal legal drug in America. It is the chemical equivalent of the drug Ecstasy. It is an amphetamine, an upper.

Do you remember the drug Fen Phen? It was taken off the market because there seemed to be some serious side effects, including heart conditions. Fen Phen is a serotonin enhancer and an amphetamine. Its pharmaceutical mechanisms are the same as Prozac's, the same as Ecstasy's.

---

[7] Greenberg, G., (2001, July). *The Serotonin Surprise. Discover Magazine*, 64-68.

When you do not like yourself, start comparing yourself to others and find you are not the best thing since peanut butter, you start to look inward. You don't think you are fearfully and wonderfully made; you think God made a mistake.

When you begin to look inward and don't like what you see, then serotonin levels decrease. When serotonin levels decrease, it causes the rate of metabolism to also decrease. When the rate of metabolism decreases, your burn rate goes down. If your caloric intake is up over 1,900 calories, then you put on weight.

On the other hand, when you like yourself and accept yourself, serotonin levels are normal. Your rate of metabolism speeds up. The rate of caloric burn increases.

A MAN ON PROZAC

Let's talk about a guy that does not like himself very much and he never heard his daddy say, "I love you." He is not Charles Atlas, which is a good thing, but he thinks he needs to be. He just feels unsettled and yucky, which is the way someone feels when his or her serotonin levels are down.

Our friend here needs an upper. He may go into the drug culture and take uppers because he's down. Then he may find himself too high, so he may then take downers. Now he is a yo-yo. Up, down, up, down. This is the typical cycle of the drug culture.

The pharmaceutical industry also knows how to make this man feel good. He can order Prozac just by asking his doctor—just because he thinks he needs it and not for any specific medical reason. Prozac is now being prescribed more than any other drug in America.

Anyone who feels down can call their doctor and say, "I have a yucky feeling."

The response they get is, "I've got a great drug for you: Prozac."

According to the PDR, anxiety is the first side effect of Prozac. Our friend in my little story did not like himself very much before and now he feels a little better about himself. But he is looking over his shoulder in paranoia all the time about everything in life.

Another major side effect is loss of libido, or sex drive. Now you have a guy who likes himself a little better and has anxiety, but he loses all interest in his wife.

A man who loses interest in his wife might as well go sit on the roof! One thing I have learned about being married is my wife wants to be pursued and I am not talking sexually—I am talking about luring her heart. I am talking about letting her know she is special.

I can see my wife across the room and give her just one "look" and she will blush, turn red and melt. One look and she is gone; but I have earned the right to go there. She has been designed by God to be a responder in the marital relationship. If a husband loses interest in his wife, which is what loss of libido does, there is trouble coming!

Now let's look at some common side effects of the drug Prozac.

PROZAC'S SIDE EFFECTS

allergic reaction

anxiety

chest pain

chills

coughing

diarrhea

dizziness

drowsiness

dry mouth

flu symptoms

frequent urination

hay fever

headache

inability to fall or stay asleep

increased appetite

indigestion

intestinal disorders

joint pain

nausea

sore throat

sweating

tremors

weakness

weight loss

abnormal thinking: "Yes, I feel better about myself—I just can't think straight."

loss of libido

sexual dysfunction

abnormal gait: "Yes, I feel better about myself, but I just can't walk a straight line. I don't know why."

amnesia: "Yes, I feel better about myself, but I have forgotten who I am."

apathy

confusion

convulsions

fluttery heartbeat

hair loss

hallucinations

hostility

paranoid reactions

twitching

Rarer side effects include antisocial behavior, extreme muscle tension, slurred speech, stupor, suicidal thoughts and, occasionally, cessation of breathing.

Our friend from my illustration may feel better about himself, but at what cost?

Neurogenesis

Something else in *Discover* Magazine really got my attention. It is called neurogenesis: a regeneration of certain brain cells.

I learned something about God and I learned something about the enemy. We have known that brain cells do not regenerate, nerve tissue does not regenerate and organ tissue does not regenerate. However, there is evidence some brain cell regeneration can occur. Certain types of nerve tissue can regenerate. Even recently in medical research, they have discovered heart tissue can, to some degree, regenerate itself if it does not continue to be diseased.

That was encouraging to me in ministry!

Scientists have found that neurogenesis occurs in the hippocampus, the part of the brain associated with learning, memory and, perhaps, emotion. Neurogenesis means the continued remanufacturing of neurons that are responsible for memory and emotion. This neurogenesis works when you feel good about yourself, as long as serotonin levels are at the proper valuation. When you do not like yourself, serotonin levels begin to dip. Then you lose your ability to maintain memory and emotional stability. You go into a certain low-grade degree of confusion.

Now here is what they have discovered. Since Prozac is a serotonin enhancer, if you take it, you do not need peace anymore. You do not need to like yourself anymore. You do not need to have your peace with God, your wife or your mother-in-law. You just need Prozac.

41

Prozac causes serotonin to stay in circulation longer, creating neurogenesis, which is a by-product of serotonin levels being normal. We have become a nation of zombies. We don't need God anymore. We don't need righteousness or sanctification anymore. We don't need to feel good about ourselves anymore. We just need Prozac.

This magazine points out that street drugs are much more carefully scrutinized for potential harmful effects than are pharmaceutical drugs. The author of the article believes fewer drugs and more therapy would be advisable. In other words, many of the people taking serotonin-enhancing drugs would respond just as well to "talk therapy" as to a drug.

Well, that almost sounds scriptural! You have to be careful that Satan does not counterfeit God, even in Christianity. The Bible says to "confess your faults one to another so that you may be healed." We are in trouble!

> Confess *your* faults one to another, and pray one for another, that ye may be healed. The effectual fervent prayer of a righteous man availeth much.
>
> James 5:16

Conclusion

If you are taking prescription drugs, think about why you do it.

Just because you have been exposed to this information, *please do not come off any prescription drugs because you now feel guilty.* I must put a disclaimer in here: I will not interfere with you and your physician. I am a pastor administering the Scriptures.

Do not ever come off any prescription drug without constant observation and administration by your physician. You have a right to apply your heart before God and let Him work with you. He is not in a hurry!

Do not ever come off any drug without help from your doctor

Some people say, "Well, God told me to come off my medication."

If God told you to come off your medication, that is between you and God. I would not interfere with you, but I would make sure it was God talking to you! You have a right to apply your heart before God and let Him work with you. This means God gives you His mercy—which is a measure of time—to walk this thing out.

However, I want you to be aware of something very important. A drug creates an altered chemical state of reality in your body and will program your body to want it. By taking a drug, you have created an altered chemical state in your body and your body has now become familiar with it.

43

Your body will require that chemistry to be maintained. So to retrain your body will take some time of withdrawal. You will have to reprogram your body chemically to be able to exist without the drug.

Don't go into guilt from information like this! Simply go before Father God and ask Him to begin to show you *a more excellent way*™ so that you can recover yourself from the snare of the devil.

> And *that* they may recover themselves out of the snare of the devil, who are taken captive by him at his will.
>
> 2 Timothy 2:26